COMPOSER SHOWCASE
HAL LEONARD STUDENT PIANO LIBRARY

EARLY ADVANCED LEVEL

Three Preludes

A MYTHICAL TRIPTYCH FOR PIANO SOLO

BY CHRISTOS TSITSAROS

Commissioned by the Wisconsin Music Teachers Association and MTNA.

CONTENTS

2   *Performance Notes*

5   Prelude no. 1
    Water Nymphs

12 Prelude no. 2
    Dance Mystique

20 Prelude no. 3
    Dionysian Rites

ISBN 978-1-4803-9678-4

HAL•LEONARD®
CORPORATION

7777 W. BLUEMOUND RD. P.O. BOX 13819 MILWAUKEE, WI 53213

In Australia Contact:
Hal Leonard Australia Pty. Ltd.
4 Lentara Court
Cheltenham, Victoria, 3192 Australia
Email: ausadmin@halleonard.com.au

Visit Hal Leonard Online at
www.halleonard.com

Performance Notes

Greek mythology forms part of our ancestors' cultural and intellectual heritage to the world. Unlike other religions, Greeks attributed human qualities and faults to their gods in a way that in their myths, mortals could identify themselves and learn from the gods' interactions and conflicts. Not only do Greek myths mirror everyday life, they also provide an insight to natural phenomena, the origin of humankind, and the unfathomable depth of the human soul.

The present three preludes endeavor to capture the imaginative spirit, colorful pictorial aspect, and mystical meaning of these myths.

The first prelude *(Water Nymphs)*, evokes the nimble dancing and singing of the water nymphs, divine graceful spirits, who animated nature and gave birth to immortal children. Water nymphs included the Nereids, who resided in the Mediterranean Sea, the Naiads, who bathed in fresh water and were regarded as protectors of young maidens, as well as the Oceanides, who were usually found in salty water. Play this piece with a light, dreamy and colorful sound, interspersed with brighter, more luminous touches (as in mm. 17, 25, and 26). The middle section (mm. 27-41), driven by its robust rhythmic energy and increasing dynamic intensity, culminates in a largely sonorous climactic point (mm. 33-39). The tempo should optimally remain steady throughout the ending section (m. 52-end), as the irregular fragmentation of the motive resounds hauntingly and obsessively against the fluid accompaniment.

Ceremonial dances were traditionally integrated into different mysteries, such as the Eleusinian mysteries (held in honor of Demeter–the goddess of agriculture and fertility), or the mysteries held in Delphi, at the sanctuary of Apollo–the god of light, music, and poetry. Such ceremonies and festivals included animal sacrifices, athletic and poetic contests, as well as theatrical productions. The second prelude *(Dance Mystique)* is suggestive of the enigmatic quality associated with the Delphic oracle and the shrouded atmosphere of the ceremonies. Let the opening phrase unfold peacefully, in a flexible, expressive *cantabile*. Measures 21-36 are more dance-like, therefore employ a light bounce and a tighter rhythmical structure. The ensuing tumultuous, *più agitato* section (mm. 37-76) is fiercely dramatic and impassioned. The sweeping figurations are best supported by applications of long pedal. The resulting overtones should carry through the transition back to the tranquil mood of the opening (mm. 76-125). Allow the sound to die away in the ending section (mm.146-end), while sensitively layering the texture and maintaining the continuity of the line.

The third prelude *(Dionysian Rites)* was inspired by the exuberant and boisterous character of the Dionysian rites, in which participants were induced to an ecstatic trance state through music, dance, and the consumption of wine, the effects of which were attributed to the possession of the god's own spirit. Based on the themes of seasonal birth and rebirth, and celebrating god Dionysus' embodiment of fertility, the aim of the mysteries was to liberate the individual and lead cult practitioners to a primordial source of being, with all the associated invigorating, and transformative effects. Perform this piece in a vivid, energetic tempo, but not overly fast. The relentless, impetuous drive of the first section contrasts with the darker majestic mood of the middle section (mm. 24-50), suggestive of the transcendental undertones of the rites. Deliver the ever-expanding phrase of the middle section in a slightly more relaxed pace, with a lavishly rich yet sustained sound, while maintaining a steady motion in the underlying *ostinato*. The passionate final section is suggestive of the liberating exaltation that the rites were meant to elicit. The brilliantly resonant effect of the rapid arpeggiations against the broad *fortissimo* chords should transport the listener to the times of this captivating and enthralling mythological scene.

This work is dedicated to the loving memory of Carol Klose,
whose enormous compositional talent, kindness, and friendship
has supported and inspired me throughout the years.
She serves as a measure of excellence and a worthy example to follow.

Prelude no. 1
Water Nymphs

Christos Tsitsaros

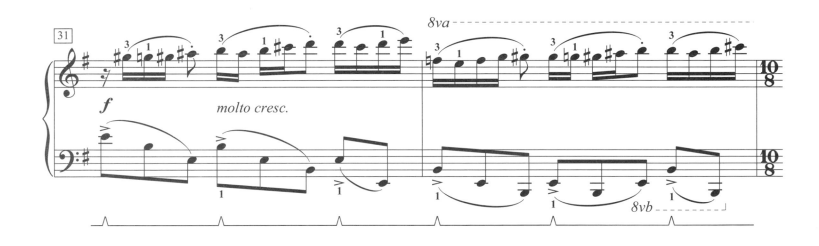

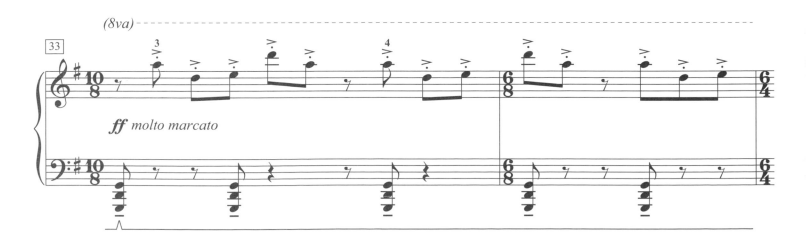

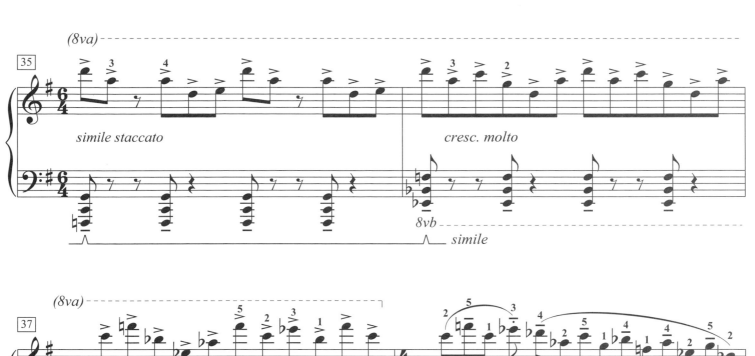

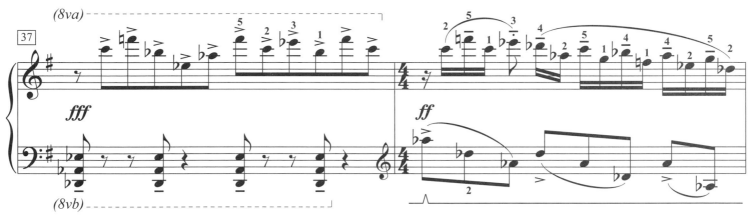

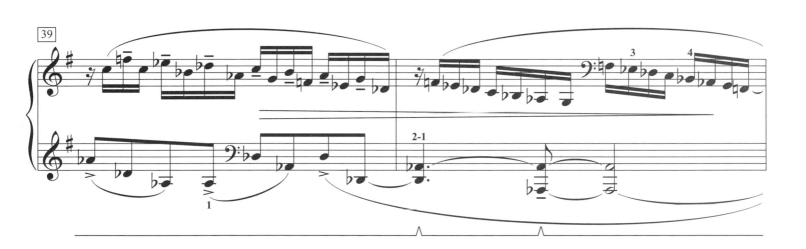

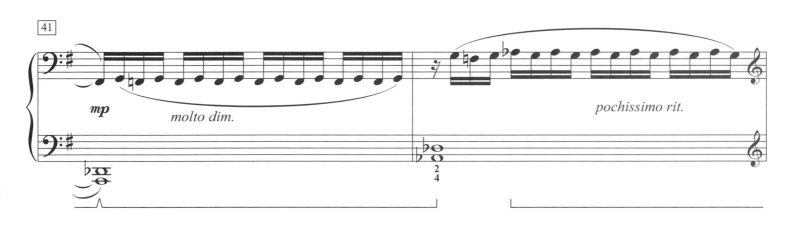

Prelude no. 2

Dance Mystique

Christos Tsitsaros

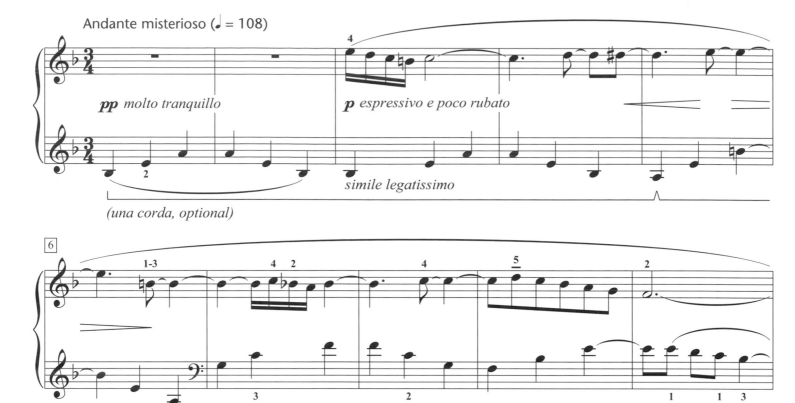

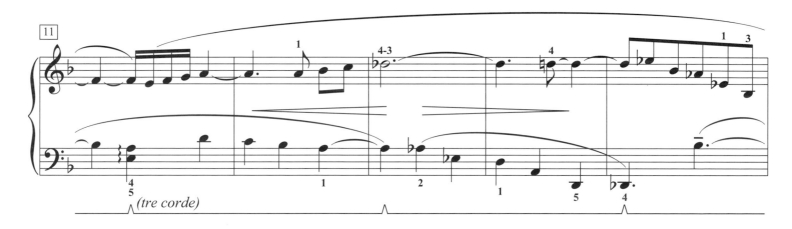

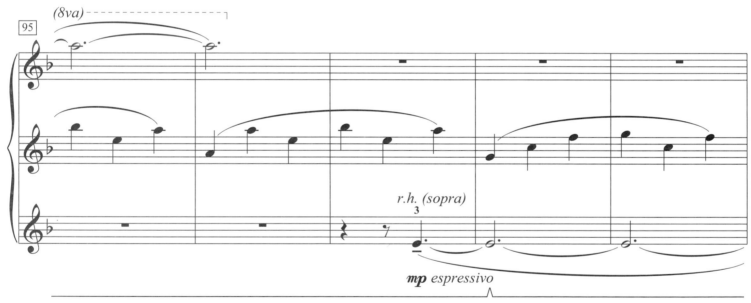

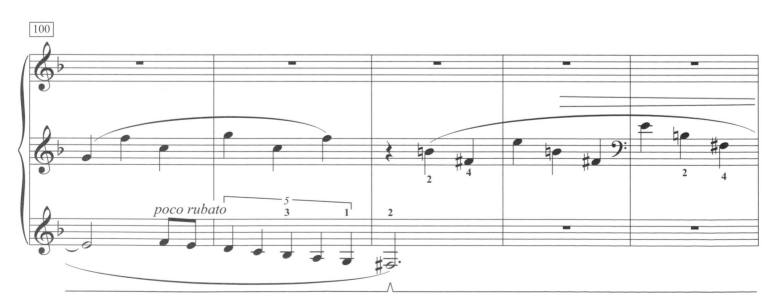

19

Prelude no. 3

Dionysian Rites

Christos Tsitsaros

Allegro con spirito (♩ = 132)

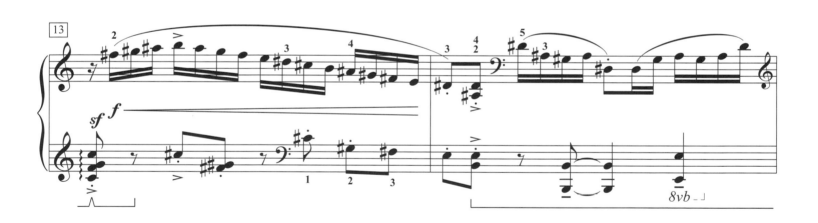

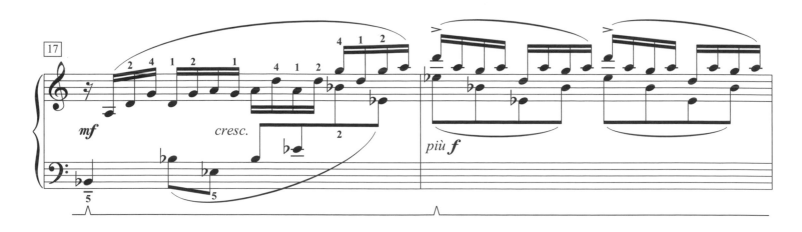

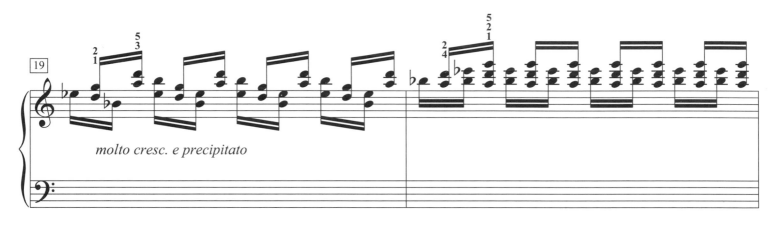

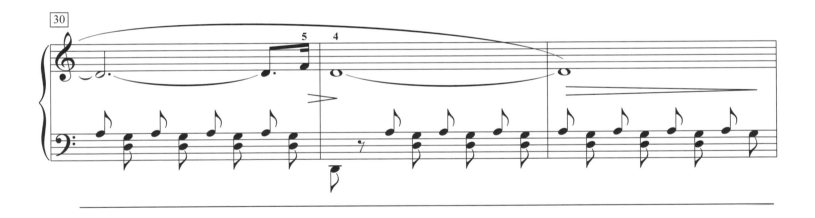

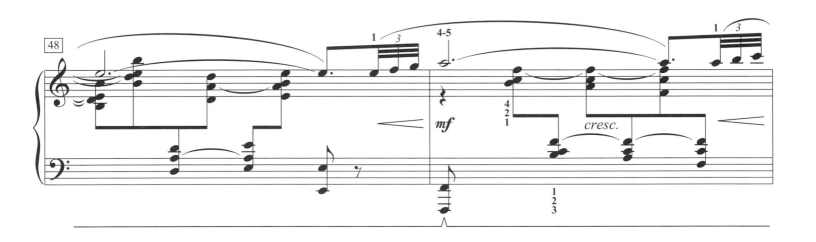

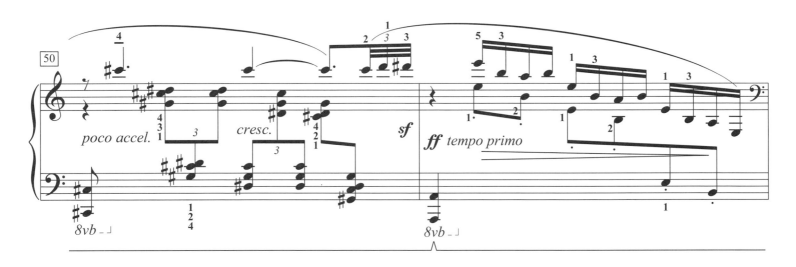

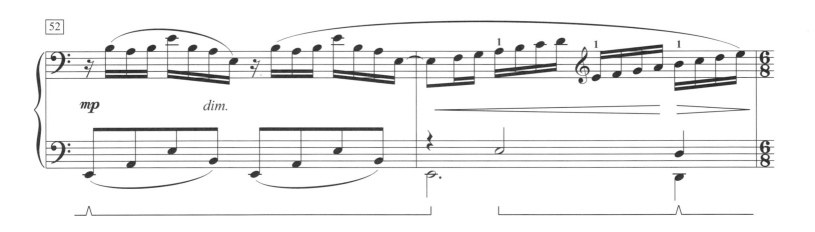

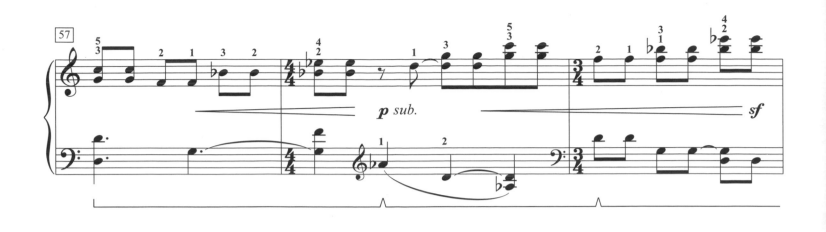

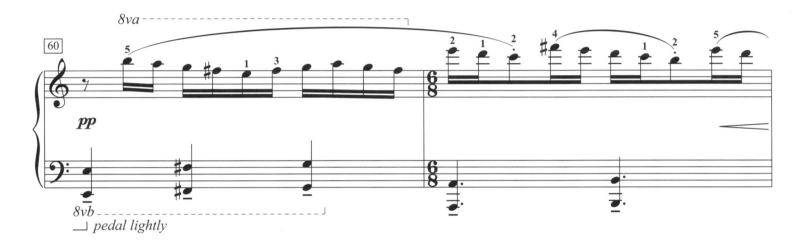

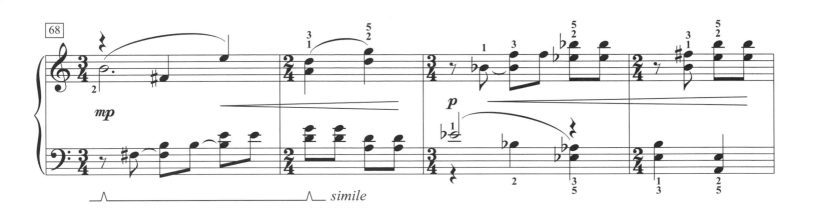

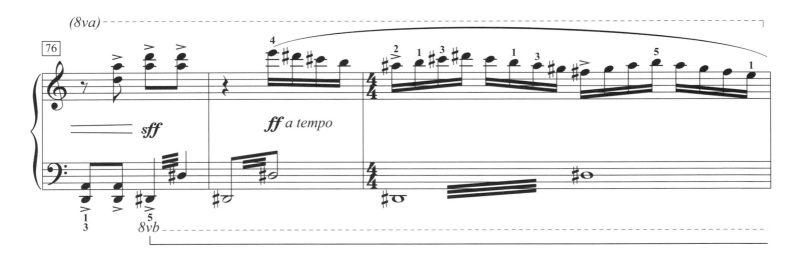

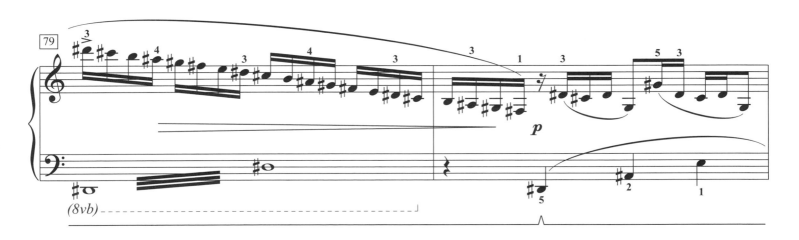

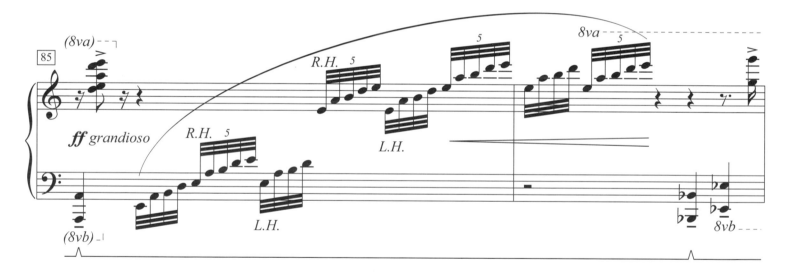

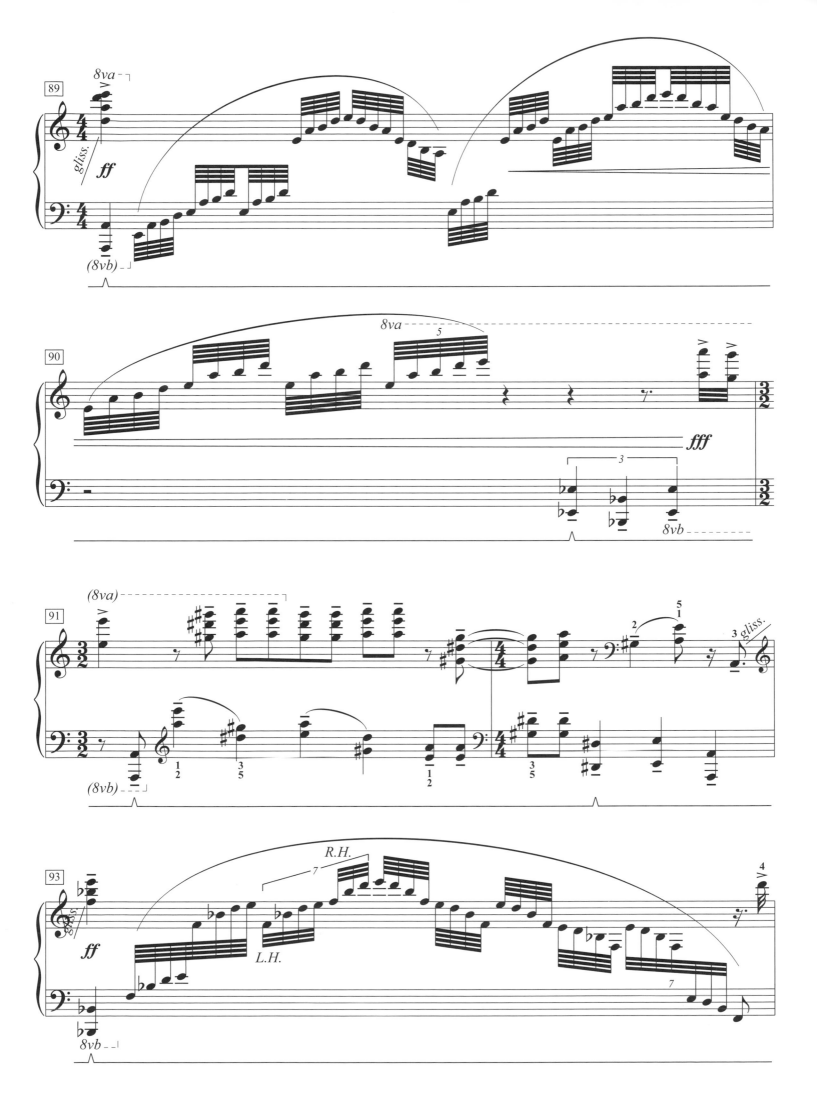

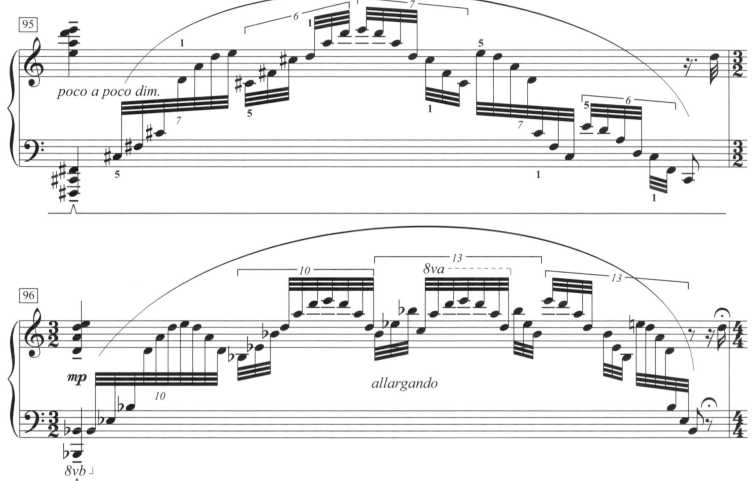

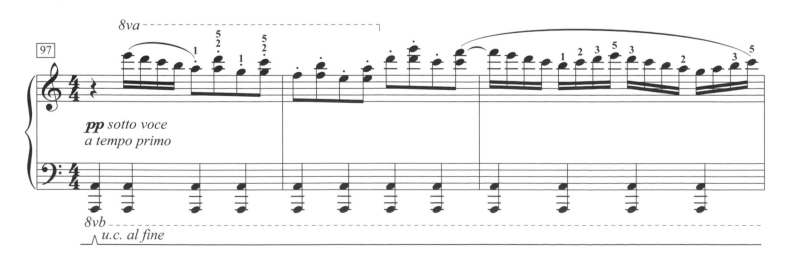

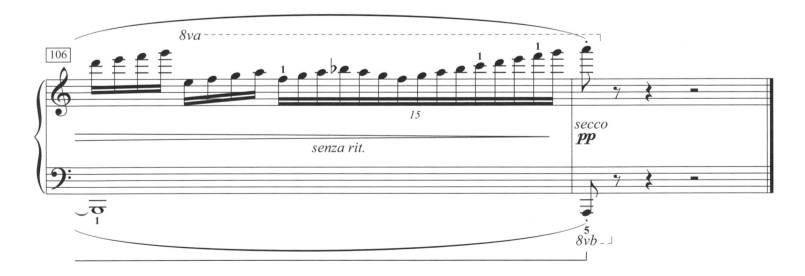

COMPOSER SHOWCASE
HAL LEONARD STUDENT PIANO LIBRARY

This series showcases great original piano music from our **Hal Leonard Student Piano Library** family of composers, including Bill Boyd, Phillip Keveren, Carol Klose, Jennifer Linn, Mona Rejino, Eugénie Rocherolle and more. Carefully graded for easy selection, each book contains gems that are certain to become classics!

BILL BOYD

JAZZ BITS (AND PIECES)
Early Intermediate Level
00290312 11 Solos..........................$7.99

JAZZ DELIGHTS
Intermediate Level
00240435 11 Solos..........................$7.99

JAZZ FEST
Intermediate Level
00240436 10 Solos..........................$7.99

JAZZ PRELIMS
Early Elementary Level
00290032 12 Solos..........................$6.99

JAZZ SKETCHES
Intermediate Level
00220001 8 Solos............................$7.99

JAZZ STARTERS
Elementary Level
00290425 10 Solos..........................$6.99

JAZZ STARTERS II
Late Elementary Level
00290434 11 Solos..........................$7.99

JAZZ STARTERS III
Late Elementary Level
00290465 12 Solos..........................$7.99

THINK JAZZ!
Early Intermediate Level
00290417 Method Book.....................$10.99

DEBORAH BRADY

PUPPY DOG TALES
Elementary Level
00296718 5 Solos............................$6.95

TONY CARAMIA

JAZZ MOODS
Intermediate Level
00296728 8 Solos............................$6.95

SUITE DREAMS
Intermediate Level
00296775 4 Solos............................$6.99

SONDRA CLARK

DAKOTA DAYS
Intermediate Level
00296521 5 Solos............................$6.95

FAVORITE CAROLS FOR TWO
Intermediate Level
00296530 5 Duets...........................$7.99

FLORIDA FANTASY SUITE
Intermediate Level
00296766 3 Duets...........................$7.95

ISLAND DELIGHTS
Intermediate Level
00296666 4 Solos............................$6.95

THREE ODD METERS
Intermediate Level
00296472 3 Duets...........................$6.95

For full descriptions and song lists for the books listed here, and to view a complete list of titles in this series, please visit our website at www.halleonard.com

MATTHEW EDWARDS

CONCERTO FOR YOUNG PIANISTS
FOR 2 PIANOS, FOUR HANDS
Intermediate Level Book/CD
00296356 3 Movements $16.95

CONCERTO NO. 2 IN G MAJOR
FOR 2 PIANOS, 4 HANDS
Intermediate Level Book/CD
00296670 3 Movements....................$16.95

PHILLIP KEVEREN

MOUSE ON A MIRROR
Late Elementary Level
00296361 5 Solos............................$6.95

MUSICAL MOODS
Elementary/Late Elementary Level
00296714 7 Solos............................$5.95

ROMP!
A DIGITAL KEYBOARD ENSEMBLE FOR SIX PLAYERS
Intermediate Level
00296549 Book/CD..........................$9.95

SHIFTY-EYED BLUES
Late Elementary Level
00296374 5 Solos............................$6.99

TEX-MEX REX
Late Elementary Level
00296353 6 Solos............................$6.99

CAROL KLOSE

CORAL REEF SUITE
Late Elementary Level
00296354 7 Solos............................$6.99

DESERT SUITE
Intermediate Level
00296667 6 Solos............................$7.99

FANCIFUL WALTZES
Early Intermediate Level
00296473 5 Solos............................$7.95

GARDEN TREASURES
Late Intermediate Level
00296787 5 Solos............................$7.99

ROMANTIC EXPRESSIONS
Intermediate/Late Intermediate Level
00296923 5 Solos............................$8.99

WATERCOLOR MINIATURES
Early Intermediate Level
00296848 7 Solos............................$7.99

JENNIFER LINN

AMERICAN IMPRESSIONS
Intermediate Level
00296471 6 Solos............................$7.99

CHRISTMAS IMPRESSIONS
Intermediate Level
00296706 8 Solos............................$6.99

JUST PINK
Elementary Level
00296722 9 Solos............................$6.99

LES PETITES IMAGES
Late Elementary Level
00296664 7 Solos............................$7.99

LES PETITES IMPRESSIONS
Intermediate Level
00296355 6 Solos............................$7.99

REFLECTIONS
Late Intermediate Level
00296843 5 Solos............................$7.99

TALES OF MYSTERY
Intermediate Level
00296769 6 Solos............................$7.99

MONA REJINO

CIRCUS SUITE
Late Elementary Level
00296665 5 Solos............................$5.95

JUST FOR KIDS
Elementary Level
00296840 8 Solos............................$7.99

MERRY CHRISTMAS MEDLEYS
Intermediate Level
00296799 5 Solos............................$7.99

PORTRAITS IN STYLE
Early Intermediate Level
00296507 6 Solos............................$7.99

EUGÉNIE ROCHEROLLE

ENCANTOS ESPAÑOLES
(SPANISH DELIGHTS)
Intermediate Level
00125451 6 Solos............................$7.99

JAMBALAYA
FOR 2 PIANOS, 8 HANDS
Intermediate Level
00296654 Piano Ensemble.................$9.99

JAMBALAYA
FOR 2 PIANOS, 4 HANDS
Intermediate Level
00296725 Piano Duo (2 Pianos)........$7.95

TOUR FOR TWO
Late Elementary Level
00296832 6 Duets...........................$7.99

TREASURES
Late Elementary/Early Intermediate Level
00296924 7 Solos............................$8.99

CHRISTOS TSITSAROS

DANCES FROM AROUND THE WORLD
Early Intermediate Level
00296688 7 Solos............................$6.95

LYRIC BALLADS
Intermediate/Late Intermediate Level
00102404 6 Solos............................$8.99

POETIC MOMENTS
Intermediate Level
00296403 8 Solos............................$8.99

SONATINA HUMORESQUE
Late Intermediate Level
00296772 3 Movements $6.99

SONGS WITHOUT WORDS
Intermediate Level
00296506 9 Solos............................$7.95

THROUGHOUT THE YEAR
Late Elementary Level
00296723 12 Duets.........................$6.95

ADDITIONAL COLLECTIONS

ALASKA SKETCHES
by Lynda Lybeck-Robinson
Early Intermediate Level
00119637 8 Solos............................$7.99

AMERICAN PORTRAITS
by Wendy Stevens
Intermediate Level
00296817 6 Solos............................$7.99

AT THE LAKE
by Elvina Pearce
Elementary/Late Elementary Level
00131642 10 Solos and Duets.............$7.99

COUNTY RAGTIME FESTIVAL
by Fred Kern
Intermediate Level
00296882 7 Rags............................$7.99

PLAY THE BLUES!
by Luann Carman (Method Book)
Early Intermediate Level
00296357 10 Solos..........................$9.99

HAL•LEONARD®
CORPORATION

7777 W. BLUEMOUND RD. P.O. BOX 13819 MILWAUKEE, WI 53213

0814